Mastering Media

Advertising Attack

Laura J. Hensley

Chicago, Illinois

www.heinemannraintree.com
Visit our website to find out more information about Heinemann-Raintree books.

To order:
☎ Phone 888-454-2279
🖳 Visit www.heinemannraintree.com to browse our catalog and order online.

Edited by Adam Miller, Andrew Farrow, and Adrian Vigliano
Designed by Steve Mead
Original illustrations © Capstone Global Library Ltd.
Picture research by Elizabeth Alexander
Production by Alison Parsons
Originated by Capstone Global Library Ltd.
Printed and bound by South China Printing Company Ltd.

14 13 12 11 10
10 9 8 7 6 5 4 3 2 1

Library of Congress Cataloging-in-Publication Data
Hensley, Laura.
 Advertising Attack / Laura J. Hensley.—1st ed.
  p. cm.—(Mastering media)
 Includes bibliographical references and index.
  ISBN 978-1-4109-3842-8 (hc)
1. Advertising. 2. Advertising campaigns.
I. Title. 0
 HF5823.H356 2010
 659.1—dc22
2010003445

Acknowledgments
We would like to thank the following for permission to reproduce photographs: Alamy p. **34** (© Donald Nausbaum); CARTOON NETWORK and all related characters and elements are trademarks of Cartoon Network © 2010. A Time Warner Company. All Rights Reserved p. **42**; Corbis pp. **4** (© Doug Pearson/JA), **16** (© Leon/Retna Ltd.), **18** (© Robert Landau), **20** (© John Van Hasselt/Sygma) **36** (© A3502_Horst Ossinger/dpa), **40** (© Denis Balibouse/Reuters); © DACS 2010 p. **8** (Alamy/INTERFOTO); Getty Images pp. **6** (Hulton Archive), **10** (Jon Feingersh/Iconica), **12** (SW Productions/Photodisc), **14** (Commercial Eye/Iconica), **23** (Pierre Tostee/ALLSPORT), **31** (Tim Boyle), **35** (WireImage/Eamonn McCormack), **39** (Scott Gries); IGA Worldwide p. **41**; Image courtesy of The Advertising Archives pp. **17**, **21**, **24**, **26**, **29**, **30**; Photolibrary p. **32** (Tao Gan/Iconotec); Shutterstock p. **46** (© Netfalls).

Cover photograph of Times Square and advertising signs, reproduced with permission of Corbis/© Jose Fuste Raga.

We would like to thank Devorah Heitner for her invaluable help in the preparation of this book.

Contents

Some words are printed in bold, **like this**. You can find out what they mean by looking in the glossary.

Advertising All Around You

Visitors to New York City's Times Square are surrounded by advertising.

Y ou may not realize it, but advertising is a central part of your daily life. Advertising is the way that products and services are introduced to the public—for example, through a television commercial or billboard. Studies suggest that you see as many as 5,000 advertising messages a day!

Over the course of a typical day, you may see print ads in newspapers or magazines, commercials on television, ads on the Internet, e-mail ads, ads on the sides of buses, billboards, posters, and even ads in video games. There are also many kinds of ads that do not look like ads at all, like when a character in a movie drinks a certain brand of soda.

How does advertising affect you?

But what is the effect of all this advertising? Some people argue that advertising is a good thing. It helps people learn about all their options before they spend their money. It also helps sell products and services, which creates jobs and keeps the economy moving.

Other people have concerns, however. They worry that advertising makes people constantly want items that they do not need and possibly cannot afford to buy. Some kinds of advertising—for example, for tobacco—support unhealthy lifestyle choices. Studies also show that people's self-image is sometimes affected by feeling they do not measure up to the people with perfect lives they see in advertising.

Become a savvy consumer

As you read this book, you will learn how advertising works. Advertisers use **strategies**, techniques, and tricks that are meant to make you want to buy things. By understanding what an advertisement is doing and how it is meant to affect you, you will become a **savvy consumer**.

Advertising will probably always be a part of your life, but it is up to you to decide how you let it affect your choices.

A Brief History of Advertising

This is an advertisement for soap from the late 1800s. What about this ad would work, or not work, today?

Throughout history, people have created basic forms of advertising, such as signs. However, advertising did not become the big business we think of today until the Industrial Revolution. This was a period, flourishing in the 1800s, when machines and factories became widely used.

Advertising's beginnings

Before the Industrial Revolution, most of what people bought was available at local stores. They also made many things and grew and raised food for themselves. But new factories allowed huge numbers of items to be created and sold. The rise of rail transportation allowed these goods to be sent to faraway places. People began to function more as **consumers** instead of producers.

People had a wide range of products to buy, from food to soap to clothes. Early advertisers began to use **broadsides**, **trade cards**, and **handbills** to make people aware of their products.

During the Industrial Revolution, new printing presses made newspapers and magazines much more affordable and widely available. These were obvious places for companies to advertise their products, but a system was not yet in place to do so.

As a result, the first important **advertising agencies** developed in the mid-1800s. The people in these agencies sold "space" in newspapers and magazines to companies that wanted to advertise.

Creating brand names

Up until the mid-1800s, local stores had unmarked bins filled with products. However, by the 1880s many companies began to put their name and **logo** on small packages that could be bought individually. People became aware of these products from advertisements. People began valuing well-known brand names, as they do today. Powerful brands such as Campbell's Soup, Quaker Oats, and Coca-Cola developed widely known brand names during this period.

LBo

DAMENSTRÜMPFE

In the 1920s advertisers focused on selling items to young women, known as flappers, who were interested in buying the newest fashions.

A big business

By 1900, large advertising agencies began to form. These agencies hired people who specialized in creating words and images for advertisements (see pages 12 and 13). Agencies also began to understand the importance of researching the likes and needs of a product's **target audience**.

Traditional advertising **media** such as newspapers remained popular during the first part of the 1900s, along with billboards and posters. In the 1920s, radio began to develop as a new medium for advertising.

Difficult times

During the 1930s, people lived through a period called the Great Depression. Many people had very little money to spend. As a result, advertisers struggled.

Later, during World War II (1939–45), advertisers spent much of their time supporting the war effort with posters, radio advertisements, and print advertisements. This kind of advertising is called **propaganda**. It means using the techniques of advertising to make people believe in a political cause.

Advertising's golden age

After the war, during the 1950s, New York City's Madison Avenue became the center of several important, powerful advertising agencies. Their big **budgets** and bold ideas made advertising enter everyday life more than ever before.

People came to desire a "perfect life" filled with products like the cars and appliances they saw in advertisements. Television became the newest way for advertisers to spread their message during this period.

Changing times

During the 1960s and 1970s, powerful advertising agencies also began to form in the United Kingdom and Europe. There and in the United States, people began to question established rules in society. This was also true in advertising, and a period of great creativity began. Attention-grabbing and playful advertisements became increasingly common (see page 24).

Recent history

The later 1980s and the 1990s were another time of great wealth. Advertising reflected this, with big-budget worldwide **advertising campaigns**. The rise of cable television also gave advertisers more ways to reach consumers.

In recent years, it has become harder for advertisers to get consumers' attention, as people increasingly "tune out" advertising. As a result, advertisers are coming up with new techniques, ranging from **place-based advertising** to "hidden" ads (see pages 33 to 41). The Internet is also being explored as a powerful new medium (see pages 43 to 45).

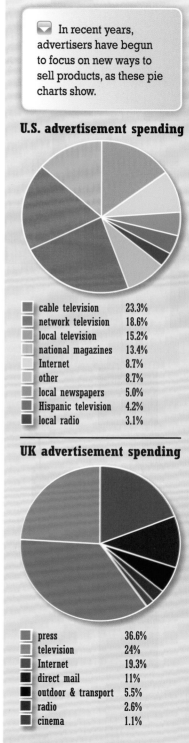

In recent years, advertisers have begun to focus on new ways to sell products, as these pie charts show.

U.S. advertisement spending

cable television	23.3%
network television	18.6%
local television	15.2%
national magazines	13.4%
Internet	8.7%
other	8.7%
local newspapers	5.0%
Hispanic television	4.2%
local radio	3.1%

UK advertisement spending

press	36.6%
television	24%
Internet	19.3%
direct mail	11%
outdoor & transport	5.5%
radio	2.6%
cinema	1.1%

How Is an Advertisement Made?

This man is "pitching," or presenting, his ideas for an advertisement to his coworkers at an advertising agency.

There are many different kinds of advertising, ranging from small-scale local advertisements to worldwide **advertising campaigns**. When a lot of money is being spent to sell a product or service, companies usually hire **advertising agencies** to help get the word out.

Finding an audience

Before creating an advertisement for a product or service, an advertising agency must do research to find its **target audience**, meaning the specific people it wants to reach. It will try to learn details about this audience such as its race, gender, age, average income, geographical location, and interests.

The agency might then show the product to a **focus group**. These are people from the target audience who are paid to tell their opinions. By learning what these people like about the product, the agency learns even more about how to appeal to them.

For example, if a company has a new type of athletic shoe, research might show that teenage boys in cities are particularly interested in these kinds of shoes. The advertiser will want to do all it can to appeal to this group. These boys' opinions will influence choices like the location, music, actors, or perhaps celebrities that are used in the advertisements.

Choosing a strategy

An advertiser needs to think about what **strategies** work best on its target audience. (See pages 15 to 23 for more on strategies.) It also needs to make itself stand apart from the competition.

In the case of the new athletic shoe, an advertiser would probably choose the strategy of playing to people's need to be admired and fit in. Advertisers know that children and teens have **insecurities** and want to be popular. The advertiser might create a sense that all the cool kids will have this new shoe.

Who's who in an advertising agency?

These are the people who work together in an advertising agency to bring an ad to life:

- **Account executive** (or account manager): This person helps the client (the company that makes the product or service) communicate its needs to the advertising agency.
- **Account planner**: This person is responsible for creating the overall strategy for selling something.
- **Creative director**: This person is in charge of all major creative decisions.
- **Art director**: This person works on the day-to-day creative jobs, such as designing an advertisement, and helps create the overall idea for an ad.
- **Copywriter**: This person is responsible for the words in an ad and also helps create the overall idea.
- **Production**: This person does the technical work, such as preparing an ad to be printed.
- **Media planner**: This person decides which media will best reach the target audience.
- **Media buyer**: This person makes deals for how much money will be paid to place an ad in different media.

Some agencies perform all these roles, some only perform creative roles, and others only do media planning and buying.

"Advertising is the greatest art form of the twentieth century."

—Marshall McLuhan, thinker

Creating the advertising campaign

Once the advertising agency has decided on its strategy, it has to decide which **media** to pursue. An advertising campaign usually includes many media. This might include print ads, television commercials, billboards, posters, direct mail (also called junk mail), Internet ads, and more. For each type of advertisement, a group of writers and artists works to create the best combination of words and images (see box at left).

Think about that pair of shoes you want. Are ads part of the reason why you want them?

Getting the message out

Once the advertisement is created, it is time to begin **marketing** the idea, or getting the message out. An advertiser needs to find the best places to reach its target audience.

For the new athletic shoe, magazines with high teenage readerships like *Spin* or *Sports Illustrated* would be a good bet, as would cable television networks targeted at teens like MTV. An advertiser gets the most value if a single advertising campaign can work well in other countries as well.

The advertiser then needs to buy "space." This means it pays the place where the advertisement will appear, such as the magazine or television network. In this way, advertising money is largely responsible for supporting these different media.

Money well spent

Advertising is a huge business—up to $400 billion is spent on it a year around the world. Advertisers therefore need to make the most effective ads possible to make sure a company's money is well spent.

Top 15 global advertisers for 2008

Rank	Company	Location	Description
1.	Proctor and Gamble	Cincinnati, Ohio	Manufactures a variety of goods, from cleaning supplies to diapers to razors
2.	General Motors	Detroit, Mich.	Car manufacturer
3.	Unilever	London, UK/Rotterdam, Netherlands	Manufactures a variety of goods, from foods to cleaning supplies to personal care products
4.	Ford Motor Company	Dearborn, Mich.	Car manufacturer
5.	Toyota Motor Corp.	Toyota City, Japan	Car manufacturer
6.	L'Oreal	Clichy, France	Manufactures makeup and beauty products
7.	Verizon Communications	New York, N.Y.	Broadband and telecommunications
8.	AT&T	Dallas, Tex.	Telecommunications
9.	Johnson & Johnson	New Brunswick, N.J.	Manufactures pharmaceuticals, medical devices, soaps and shampoos, and more
10.	Volkswagen Group	Wolfsburg, Germany	Car manufacturer
11.	McDonald's Corp.	Oak Brook, Ill.	Fast food
12.	Nestle	Vevey, Switzerland	Food manufacturer
13.	Honda Motor Co.	Tokyo, Japan	Car manufacturer
14.	Sony Corp.	Tokyo, Japan	Manufactures electronics, video and communications products, and more
15.	Reckitt Benckiser	Slough, Berkshire, UK	Manufactures health and personal care products

Advertising Strategies

If people only bought what they truly needed, a lot of companies would go out of business. Apart from basic food, clothing, and shelter, people do not really "need" much.

It is therefore often the job of advertisers to make **consumers** feel they "need" a product or service. They must make people think their lives would be less wonderful without the purchase.

Sometimes advertising goes beyond "need" to creating an image for a product or service. Advertisers work to make consumers feel so positive about something that they want to buy it, whether they need it or not. These positive feelings will also make a consumer choose the brand over the competition.

The importance of strategy

But how do advertisers achieve these goals? In most cases, they need to do more than simply list the facts about a product or service. Facts alone will not usually convince people to spend their hard-earned money.

Instead, advertisers create effective **strategies** for advertisements. Advertising strategies are ideas about how to sell something and get specific results. These strategies take into account why people react to certain advertising messages. They tap into people's most basic **insecurities**, desires, and emotions, as this chapter will show.

Understanding desire and belief

Advertisers do scientific research to develop the best strategies. Many **advertising agencies** consult with psychologists—people who study human behavior—to see how certain advertising strategies work. For example, psychologists might tell advertisers how and why certain images make people feel comforted.

Focus groups are another way for advertisers to study how and why people react to a product or ad. Advertisers need feedback from their customers, and future customers, if they want to create the most effective strategy.

Using the need to fit in

Advertising often shows happy people leading seemingly perfect, fulfilled lives. The goal is to make the consumer want to achieve that same perfection by buying the product. This strategy appeals to people's need to be loved and to fit in.

Solving your problems

Ads for products such as mouthwash, deodorant, acne medication, makeup, and weight-loss programs often feature the idea that someone goes unnoticed because of an appearance or personal-care problem. But after using the product, the person feels much better about himself or herself and stands out in a crowd.

Think about it: Do you know anyone whose life has changed this much because they bought one of these products? Probably not. But advertisers know to play upon people's insecurities. People will feel they "need" a product to change themselves for the better.

> **❝** The philosophy behind much advertising is based on the old observation that every man is really two men—the man he is and the man he wants to be. **❞**
>
> —William Feather, writer

Celebrities like Beyoncé can have a huge effect on a brand's sales.

Celebrity endorsement

Advertisers also tap into people's need to fit in by having celebrities promote their products. They hope consumers want to be like celebrities.

For example, if a star like Beyoncé uses a certain brand of cell phone in an ad, a young woman might feel more glamorous if she uses the same phone. In such instances, consumers base their buying choices on image, rather than on practical issues like value or quality.

Are you more likely to buy a product if a favorite star uses it? If so, why do you react this way?

CASE STUDY: "A diamond is forever"

Since 1947, diamond manufacturer De Beers has run an **advertising campaign** that shows loving young couples beginning their lives together with a diamond engagement ring.

Before De Beers's ads, the idea of a diamond engagement ring was not a popular tradition. People thought of diamonds as a luxury for the rich, and ordinary people never expected to own one. Today, thanks to these ads, many brides expect to receive a diamond engagement ring.

Two words. One lifetime.

DE BEERS

Because a diamond is forever

De Beers creates an image of love and status in its ads.

Proving your love

What has made these ads so effective? The ads suggest that all successful young couples begin their engagement with a diamond ring. This has made the rings become a **status symbol**, or a sign that someone is wealthy or important. Because of these ads, many men feel that they have to show their love with an expensive item, which they possibly cannot afford. Many women feel disappointed if they do not receive a diamond engagement ring.

What does this tell you about the power of advertising?

> " Good advertising does not just circulate information. It penetrates the public mind with desires and belief. "
>
> —Leo Burnett, advertiser

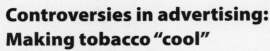

Controversies in advertising: Making tobacco "cool"

Advertisers are faced with a special challenge when trying to sell tobacco. People know that using tobacco causes illness and often death. As a result, advertisers try to sell tobacco as a lifestyle choice that will make people seem cool and even rebellious.

The Marlboro Man

In the 1950s, Marlboro needed to increase the sales of its cigarettes. It built a new image around "the Marlboro Man," a cowboy living a free, independent life in a place called Marlboro Country. Advertisements focused on rugged, handsome cowboys doing "manly" things like herding cattle. Marlboro hoped that people (especially men) living uneventful lives would want to be as free and appealing as the Marlboro Man— and, of course, buy Marlboro cigarettes, just like the Marlboro Man. The strategy worked: After one year of this campaign, the sales of Marlboro went up 3,241 percent.

Advertisers have worked to connect the image of Marlboro with rugged cowboys like this.

As a consumer, you must step back and compare the strategies in an ad like this to reality. The Marlboro Man lives an active, outdoor lifestyle. But **statistics** (numbers based on studies) show that smokers have trouble being active due to breathing problems—not to mention the enormous risks of eventually dying from cancer or heart disease. In fact, three "Marlboro Men" featured in the advertisements later died of lung cancer.

Targeting kids

Statistics show that 85 to 90 percent of smokers start in their teens. So, tobacco companies want to grab this group of customers as quickly as possible. To appeal to kids' need to fit in, advertisers promote ideas like fun, independence, and popularity.

The most obvious example of this was the Joe Camel campaign for Camel cigarettes. Beginning in 1988, a series of ads showed a cartoon camel doing "cool" things like playing pool and racing cars. Again, the strategy worked: As a result of this campaign, the percentage of U.S. smokers under 18 who smoked Camels went from under 1 percent to almost 33 percent.

Because of its effect on kids, in 1997 the U.S. government ordered that the Joe Camel campaign be stopped. However, Joe Camel is still used in ads outside the United States. The next time you see a tobacco ad, remember to focus on the reality of tobacco supported by medical and other scientific evidence—bad breath, yellow teeth, disease, and death—and not the "cool" image advertisers want to sell you.

Using emotion

Advertisers often use the strategy of emotion in advertisements. They feature ideas like a loving family, patriotism, old-fashioned values, and the innocence of children. Advertisers know that people respond warmly to these ideas. They hope that consumers will transfer these positive feelings toward the product being sold.

🔍 CASE STUDY: A "Kodak moment"

Since the 1980s, the camera and film company Kodak has used an advertising campaign showing special moments of everyday life, such as a baby's first steps. The ads say these are "Kodak moments." The strategy is to connect Kodak to the most precious moments of people's everyday lives.

> **❝ Kodak sells film, but they don't advertise film. They advertise memories. ❞**
> —Theodore Levitt, Harvard professor

These ads do not say how the film is different or better than other brands. However they do imply people are endangering their family's precious moments if they try another brand, as seen in the line: "Why trust moments like these to anything other than Kodak?"

A lasting ad
The Kodak campaign has been so effective that many people now refer to a touching scene as a "Kodak moment."

Using humor

Humor is another popular strategy in advertising. Advertisers hope that people develop positive feelings toward their product because an advertisement gave them a moment of fun.

People also tend to talk about these commercials with others, which helps spread awareness of the brand. For this reason, many popular humorous ads, such as the "Budweiser frogs," are shown during major sporting events. This way, the largest number of people are likely to see them and talk about them the next day.

 ## CASE STUDY: The Cadbury gorilla

Does it seem strange that a drum-playing gorilla made people buy a brand of chocolate?

Beginning in 2007, Cadbury, a chocolate company, had a very successful humorous advertising campaign featuring a gorilla (actually, a man in a very  believable gorilla suit). Most memorably, a television commercial featured the gorilla passionately playing the drums to Phil Collins's song "In the Air Tonight." The campaign was also used in other **media**, such as print ads and billboards.

Interestingly, the advertisements said nothing about the quality or taste of the chocolate. They were all about making people laugh and feel positively about Cadbury. This was important, as Cadbury had recently suffered bad news coverage after problems with some of its products.

People did react very positively to the gorilla advertisements. Sales of the Cadbury chocolate featured in the ad went up 9 percent. People also talked a lot about the ads, making them go **"viral"** (see pages 35 and 45).

 Generics

When you shop for most food products and household goods, you will see popular brands alongside generic products. Generic products have plain labels and receive no advertising. Studies show that many people feel more comfortable buying a name brand. They feel familiar with its image through advertising—even though the generic product is often nearly identical and up to 40 percent cheaper. This shows the power of good branding.

Each time you see an ad, write down the strategy or strategies that the advertisers used. Do you think it's an effective ad? Why or why not?

Strategy spy

Flip through a magazine and look at the ads. What strategies are they using?

Branding

One of the most powerful strategies used by advertisers is **branding**. *Branding* means creating a strong image for a product. The goal is to make people so comfortable with a product that they would not consider buying the competition.

For example, Kimberly-Clark, the company that makes Kleenex, has been very successful at branding. When people need a piece of facial tissue, they often say they need a Kleenex. They think only of the Kleenex brand, even though it is no different from many competitors' products.

Targeted branding

Sometimes branding focuses on creating a loyal **target audience**. To create this loyalty, advertisers must understand the thinking of a target audience and speak directly to them.

Think about advertisements for cars. An ad for a minivan probably shows an average-looking family and provides facts about safety and affordability. It also focuses on practical considerations such as space for groceries. This appeals to the typical minivan customer.

In contrast, an ad for a luxury sports car probably has glamorous people and focuses on issues like sophistication. This attracts a wealthy consumer who thinks about glamour and status symbols.

CASE STUDY: Mountain Dew

For many years, Mountain Dew soda was mostly popular with middle-aged people. However, in 1993 it decided to become a hip brand targeted at boys and young men.

Mountain Dew ads, such as the one on this surfer's shirt, create a sense of rebellion and fun for the brand.

Using the **slogan** "Do the Dew," it created a rebellious brand image in a campaign that featured, among other media, commercials with loud music, wildly moving cameras, and silly humor. Mountain Dew also started to **sponsor** extreme sports events like the X Games and the Dew Tour (named after the brand). Its name appeared on signs, posters, and more at these events.

As a result, Mountain Dew became one of the most popular drinks among U.S. boys and young men. The company went on to pursue young male consumers across the globe.

Think about it—the product did not change one bit, only the advertising did. What does this tell you about the power of branding, especially on young people?

Advertising Techniques and Tricks

This VW ad is still regarded as one of the best in the history of advertising.

Think small.

A dvertisers' two main tools are words and pictures. Over the years, they have developed many techniques and tricks for using words and pictures effectively. Sometimes advertisers use these methods simply to make a product seem appealing. But sometimes they do so to twist the truth.

Using words to inform

In the 1940s, a man named Rosser Reeves came up with the idea of the "Unique Selling Proposition" (USP). Reeves felt it is the job of advertisers to say why their product is special and worth buying. In particular, Reeves wrote, advertisers should make sure to say, "Buy this product, and you will get this specific benefit."

This technique is straightforward and informative. It tells **consumers** about important things like price, service, quality, and effectiveness. However, lists of facts and figures can seem boring and not hold people's attention.

 CASE STUDY: VW and "Think small"

In 1962 an advertisement for the Volkswagen Beetle car was groundbreaking in its effective use of words. It found a new way to provide important facts but also be fun and playful.

The reader first notices the words "Think small." This effective **slogan** plays upon the usual idea that people should "think big," making the reader want to read on, which is the key to an effective advertisement.

The ad then uses humor, making fun of the car's funny shape and tiny size. This was a big change from the grand, boastful claims in most car ads at the time. But after a series of humble, funny lines, the ad tells the consumer about the important advantages of buying the car, such as its good gas mileage, long-lasting tires, and low insurance rates.

This groundbreaking ad treated people with respect. It was friendly and informative, not boastful or tricky. As a result, the ad left consumers feeling positively about the product—and VW's sales rose.

 Regulating advertising

Throughout advertising's history, advertisers have claimed to have a right to **free speech**, or the right to speak their mind. At the same time, consumers have argued that advertisers should be held to certain standards of honesty.

In the United States, the Federal Trade Commission tries to make sure advertisements do not make false claims. If an advertisement is found to be making false claims, it can be removed, and sometimes even required to correct misleading information. However, with so many advertisements out there, many false claims go unchallenged.

Using words to deceive

As the VW example shows, the use of words in advertising can be an art form. However, advertisers have also perfected how to use words to deceive (or at least to confuse) consumers.

Regulations require a certain amount of honesty in advertising. But there is still a lot of room within these regulations to stretch the truth.

Act now!

Advertisers know that people can be pressured into action. If people think an item will sell out or a sale will not last, they are more likely to run out and buy a product. That is why many advertisements say things like "act now," "one day only," and "limited-time offer."

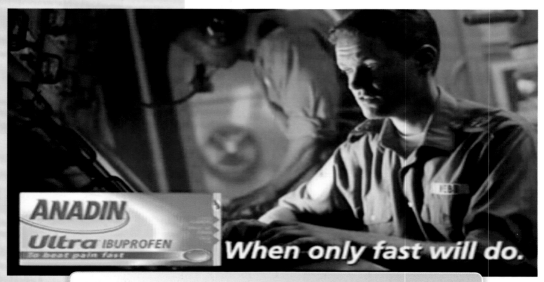

ANADIN
Ultra IBUPROFEN
To beat pain fast

When only fast will do.

What is this ad trying to tell you? It seems to be claiming that this pill acts fast. But is it the fastest-acting pill available? Maybe all pain pills claim to be fast-acting. Does the ad contain any useful information, or is it just trying to trick you without using any real data or evidence?

Weasel words

One trick that advertisers use is "weasel words," which are words that sound like they are promising something, but do not actually do so. When using weasel words, advertisers are not outright lying. Still, they knowingly create an inaccurate impression. "Weasel words" to look out for include:

- *Helps, acts, fights, supports, contributes to*, or *part of* (for example, "Supports bone health" or "Part of a healthy breakfast"): But does the product actually do this on its own?
- *Virtually, seems, looks*, or *like* (for example, "Gets windows virtually spotless"): But does the product actually do this?
- *Often, usually*, or *probably* (for example, "Users usually report noticeable results"): How often do they report these results?
- *Better* or *improved* (for example, "Better-tasting formula"): Better than what?
- *Many* or *more* (for example, "More people prefer our product over the competition"): But how many?
- Passive voice (for example, saying "It is said" as opposed to "Doctors say"): Who made this claim? If it was not an expert, it really does not matter what the person said.

> **❝** You can fool all the people all the time if the advertising is right and the **budget** is big enough. **❞**
>
> —Joseph E. Levine, filmmaker

 **Doctor recommended**

Advertisers often feature doctors or dentists in advertisements. As with studies and statistics, they hope this makes consumers think that experts support the product. However, most of the time these people are actually actors. The next time you see a medical "expert" in an ad, look for fine print explaining that it is actually an "actor portrayal."

Statistics

Advertisements often use **statistics** to prove the quality of a product. For example, "Four out of five dentists recommend this toothpaste." Advertisers hope consumers will think this kind of information sounds like scientific fact.

However, keep in mind that advertisers only report handpicked results. For example, they could have had 100 tests performed before they got the results they wanted. Yet they are not required to tell you about the first 99 tests with unfavorable results.

Studies

Advertisers use other tricks to get the results they want. For a study, they might choose a group of people who are likely to have positive feelings about their product, as opposed to a real sampling of different kinds of people.

Advertisers may also ask "leading" questions. This means questions worded to get a certain answer. For example, parents might be asked, "After reading the facts about it, would you buy this toothpaste for your family?" This would be a fair question. However, if these same people were asked, "Do you care enough about your family's dental health to buy this toothpaste?" that would be a leading question. The wording makes it seem as though parents are not concerned about their family if they do not buy the product. The question aims to get an emotional response, rather than a response based on facts and the quality of the product.

Fine print

The tiny words that appear at the bottom of print ads are called "**fine print**." Advertisers use this as a way to hide details they do not

want the consumer to notice. They will use large, noticeable words in the ad itself to say how great the product is. However the fine print will contain details like health risks or restrictions to which a special offer applies.

On television, the "fine print" sometimes appears on the screen, or sometimes a voice will read through it so quickly that it is difficult to understand.

The next time you see fine print, take the time to read it. Does reading the fine print give you a different impression of the product or service being advertised?

CAN'T TAKE THE CONGESTION?

TAKE ALLEGRA-D.

Side effects with Allegra-D were similar to Allegra alone and may include headache, insomnia, and nausea. Due to the decongestant (pseudoephedrine) component in Allegra-D, this product must not be used if you: are taking an MAO inhibitor (a medication for depression) or have stopped taking an MAO inhibitor within 14 days; retain urine; have narrow-angle glaucoma; have severe high blood pressure or severe heart disease. You should also tell your doctor if you have high blood pressure, diabetes, heart disease, glaucoma, thyroid disease, impaired kidney function, or symptoms of an enlarged prostate such as difficulty urinating. Allegra-D is for people 12 and older.

ALLEGRA-D RELIEVES YOUR MOST FRUSTRATING ALLERGY SYMPTOM: CONGESTION.

Why take an allergy decongestant that may not last as long as you want? One dose of Allegra-D lasts twice as long as one dose of the leading over-the-counter decongestant.* Talk to your doctor about Allegra-D. And don't let allergy congestion frustrate you another day.

After reading this ad's fine print, would you still use the product?

Get valuable savings @ allegra.com.
For more information call 1-800-allegra.
Please see additional important information on next page.

sanofi aventis   © 2004 Aventis Pharmaceuticals Inc. ALD JA 16258-2
Aventis Pharmaceuticals, a member of the sanofi-aventis group

allegra-D.
fexofenadine HCl 60 mg/pseudoephedrine HCl 120 mg Extended-Release Tablets
FINALLY, D-CONGESTED.

* Based on label directions. IRI data as of 5/23/04 Sudafed Maximum Strength Nasal Decongestant (4-6 hour dosage).

Using images

Advertising campaigns that use images sometimes feature beautiful photographs and creative design. For example, the VW ad on page 24 was greatly admired for its clean, elegant design. However, advertisers sometimes use images to twist the truth.

Creating beautiful people

Ads for products such as luxury goods, cosmetics, and clothes are often filled with attractive, tall, thin people. This is partly because attractive, tall, thin models and actors are hired. But there is more to the story.

> When you see a person in an ad, think about the message the ad is sending about the human body. Look at the ad below and analyze it using the "five W's" from page 31.

By using computer technology known as airbrushing, advertisers change models' features. When a print advertisement shows the slimming effects of jeans, for example, airbrushing might have been used to make the model's hips look slimmer.

Creating beauty ideals

These false images can cause serious damage. As a result of seeing so many advertisements, people come to think of the models they see as "normal." Some advertisers hope people will buy products that promise to make them match this ideal.

These ads have another effect. Some people develop

a low self-image because they do not measure up to what they see in the **media**. In extreme cases, people develop eating disorders like anorexia and bulimia to make themselves thin. As a result, some countries, such as France, want to put warning labels on airbrushed images.

Food stylists

Advertisers also use tricks to improve the appearance of food. For example, have you ever noticed that a real fast-food hamburger looks very different from the one in the ads? This is because people called food stylists glue extra sesame seeds on a bun, brush brown gravy over the meat, and choose extra-large slices of tomato. They even use some cleaning products to make food look shiny and perfect.

If a food advertisement makes your mouth water, remember that what you actually buy will not necessarily match the ad.

📷 Look more closely

When you look at an ad featuring an attractive model, break down what you think the advertiser was trying to achieve, using the "five W's":

- Who: Whom is this ad aimed at? How would the targeted person respond to this image?
- What: What does the ad show? Perhaps equally importantly, what is not shown?
- Where and When: What sort of media will show this ad? Why would the advertiser choose these media and their specific audiences?
- Why: What **strategy** would the advertiser have by choosing this sort of model and image?

By better understanding the goals of the advertiser, you might be less influenced by the ideals presented and more able to see the various strategies for what they are.

How do pictures like this one compare to the actual food you see at most fast-food restaurants?

NEW **ENORMOUS** OMELET SANDWICH

It's HUGE!

Available during breakfast hours only.

Desperate for Attention

Advertisers are always trying to find new ways to make sure you see their ads. What's the most desperate ad placement you have seen recently?

Advertising has always been focused on getting people's attention. Over the years, advertisers have used extra-loud television commercials, repetition, barely clothed models, and other techniques in an attempt to get noticed.

However, in recent years **consumers** have learned to "tune out" traditional advertising. As a result, advertisers are coming up with new ways to get people to take notice.

Place-based advertising

Advertisers are increasingly exploring **place-based advertising**. Building upon the earlier ideas of posters and billboards, this kind of advertising tries to find new places for ads where people will see them during everyday life.

Some of the more well-known examples of place-based advertising include ads on buses, ads on bus shelters, airplanes pulling banners behind them, and huge electronic signs in places like Times Square. Sports stadiums and concert venues are also covered with ads, including digital ads that can be changed.

But advertisers are coming up with stranger places all the time, such as bathroom stalls, doctors' offices, ATM screens, escalator stairs, and stickers on fruit in the supermarket. There are even billboards on wheels, called street blimps, that drive around cities. Where else have you seen advertisements popping up unexpectedly?

A captive audience?

In many instances of place-based advertising, consumers are "captive audiences." They need to stay where the ad is for a period of time—for example, as they wait for a bus. Advertisers hope people will spend time examining the ad as they wait.

But some people worry that so many advertisements ruin the beauty of cities and towns. They also worry that there might eventually be no moments in everyday life that are free of **commercialism**, or a focus on buying and selling things.

 Ambush marketing

Ambush marketing is when advertisers show up at an event **sponsored** by a competitor's product. For example, when a major sporting event is sponsored by one brand of soda, another brand may have planes fly with advertising banners overhead or have employees hand out free samples of their product.

> Guerrilla marketing has traditionally been a tool used by small businesses, as in the photo below. However, today it is increasingly common to see large companies trying guerilla marketing campaigns.

Guerrilla marketing

One of the newest ways advertisers are trying to grab attention is through **guerrilla marketing**. This means creating clever, attention-grabbing advertisements in public places. Unlike place-based advertising, guerrilla marketing usually has a much smaller **budget** and uses inexpensive **media**, like writing a message in chalk on city sidewalks. Anyone with something to sell can do it.

For example, at the 2004 Olympic Games in Athens, Greece, a man surprised the crowd at a diving competition with a guerrilla-marketing stunt. Dressed like a ballet dancer in a tutu and tights, with the name of an online gaming website painted on his chest, the man stood on the edge of the diving board and became a human billboard.

This was meant to be a funny, surprising sight and bring attention to the company. However,

several divers missed their dives because they were so thrown off by the surprise, and many people thought it was in poor taste. What effect would a guerrilla-marketing campaign like this have on you?

Going viral

Recently, advertisers have begun to make ads that are meant to go "**viral**." This means that people will talk about the ad in person and in blogs and chat rooms, which makes people want to view the ad for themselves on websites like YouTube, which then helps to spread the word about the product for free.

 CASE STUDY: T-Mobile

In 2009 T-Mobile, a cell phone service provider, had a group of 400 dancers quietly spread into the main hall of London's Liverpool Street Station during the morning commute. The dancers suddenly performed a series of choreographed dances, from hip-hop to classical. Hundreds of stunned, amused observers watched the routine, with some even joining in. The whole event was caught by hidden cameras and turned into a television commercial.

T-Mobile's ad created a youthful image for the brand.

The commercial earned T-Mobile a lot of attention and went "viral." A group of 13,000 people later organized on Facebook and showed up at the station to re-create the ad. The story of this "flash mob" was reported on major news networks throughout the world.

The ad gave the brand a sense of cool and fun. However, it said nothing specific about T-Mobile's products and services. Would you be more interested in using T-Mobile after seeing this ad? Do you think this kind of advertising works?

Is It an Ad?

Advertisers try to make the products in infomercials seem irresistible.

As we have seen, people today often ignore advertisements. Many people also resent how much advertising surrounds them. As a result, advertisers try to find ways to create "hidden" advertisements that people do not realize are advertisements at all.

Testimonial

One of the oldest kinds of hidden ads is the **testimonial**. This is when an advertisement uses the voice or words of an everyday person offering a personal story about how a product or service worked for him or her. Testimonials are used in all advertising **media**, from radio to print to billboards.

Advertisers hope that **consumers** think an everyday person, much like themselves, is offering advice that can be trusted. However, remember that these people are usually paid to make a commercial and are told what to say. It is not **objective** (purely fact-based), friendly advice.

Infomercials

Television commercials that seem like regular programming are called **infomercials**. They are usually 30 minutes long. Sometimes infomercials are made to look like a talk show or news report. They often show images of the product being used. They repeatedly provide a phone number and website where the product can be purchased.

Television networks usually show infomercials in the early-morning hours. The network must identify an infomercial as an advertisement before it starts and after it ends. However, there are also whole networks, such as the Home Shopping Network and QVC, dedicated to showing infomercials all the time.

Advertisers hope that viewers will be drawn in by what seems like regular programming. Using celebrities also helps to gain viewers' attention. When you see infomercials, remember that their goals are no different than those of traditional commercials. Also look for weasel words and other tricks (see pages 26 to 31), which are commonly used in infomercials.

Advertorials

An **advertorial** is a print advertisement that is written and designed to seem like the newspaper or magazine articles that surround it. Sometimes it will be an insert. Advertorials talk about how great a product or service is.

Advertorials are hard to spot, but they will sometimes have a small label at the top that says something like "promotional section" or

Controversies in advertising: Affecting editorial content

People assume that advertising is totally separate from the content of major media. However, this is not always the case. Major media need advertisers' money to pay their bills. This can make them willing to do what advertisers tell them to do.

Print, radio, and MTV

Newspapers and magazines are considered trusted sources of objective information. But two recent studies found that women's magazines with tobacco advertisements were less likely to write about the health risks of tobacco than magazines that did not have tobacco companies as advertisers. In other words, these magazines felt they could not criticize the people who paid them—even if that meant not warning their readers about important health risks.

When people listen to the radio, they assume the choice of songs represents the taste of the listening public and the disk jockeys. However, major record companies have regularly been accused of "payola," which means paying radio stations to play their artists. It is illegal to do this, unless there is a clear announcement that it is paid advertising time. Still, major record labels are repeatedly fined for payola.

"advertisement." You can also sometimes spot them if the text praising a product is placed opposite an ad for that same product.

Advertisers hope people will read and trust the advertorial because they think it is part of the newspaper or magazine. But remember that these are not the words of an objective, trusted writer heaping praise on a product—they are just an ad.

Movie stars like Orlando Bloom often appear on MTV to promote upcoming movies.

As part of its programming, MTV often has special shows and movie star appearances promoting upcoming movies. MTV has admitted that it only promotes a movie if the movie company has paid a lot of advertising money. The network does not make these choices because a movie is good or of interest to its viewers.

Product placement

When advertisers pay a medium such as a television show to feature their product, it is called **product placement**. For example, actors are shown drinking a certain brand of coffee. Consumers do not always realize that this is advertising. But advertisers hope consumers will be influenced by seeing their favorite stars using a product.

One of the best-known instances of product placement was in the 1982 movie *E.T.* In the film, the lovable alien E.T. was shown eating the candy Reese's Pieces. As a result of this product placement, sales of Reese's Pieces went up 65 percent. James Bond movies are also known for placing products ranging from cars to watches to vodka to cigarettes.

James Bond movies feature a lot of product placement, including images of Omega watches.

On television today, product placement is everywhere. One of the most obvious examples is *American Idol*. The judges are always shown sipping from large cups of Coke, and ads for Coke appear constantly throughout the program.

Would you have a better impression of a product if you saw it used on a favorite show?

Undercover marketing

A new kind of advertising, called **undercover marketing** or stealth marketing, makes advertising secretly enter everyday conversation. People are paid to talk up a product with people, while pretending to be everyday consumers.

For example, in 2002 Sony Ericsson Mobile paid actors to go to tourist spots in major cities. Posing as fellow tourists, they asked people to take their picture with digital cameras on Sony Ericsson phones. The idea was to let consumers see and use the new phones.

Online, advertisers pay people to say good things about a product in chat rooms and social-networking sites. Employees also leave good reviews for products on shopping websites.

In all these instances, what seems like everyday conversation is actually a paid testimonial. Many people are outraged over this. They say advertisers are **commercializing** everyday conversation. But advertisers say they are using their right to **free speech**.

Do you think you have ever encountered this technique and not realized it?

Video game product placement

Advertisers are exploring video games as a new medium for product placement. As the graphics on video games have become more advanced, companies have begun placing products in the video game environment, such as a certain brand of soda machine in a room. Some video games show characters using specific brands of cell phones, MP3 players, and more.

Advertisers are now paying to fill video games with ads and virtual product placements.

41

Internet
Advertising

The Internet is the latest major area for advertisers to explore. They are excited by what is unique about online advertising. In other advertising **media**, advertisers must choose a particular place for an ad (for example, a certain magazine). But the Internet has a much wider audience across the world.

Also, the Internet allows interaction with **consumers**. Links in advertisements lead people to different places. For example, a link can lead a consumer directly to an online store.

Advertisers can also ask people questions online. This is a free way to get the kind of information provided by **focus groups**.

Websites and e-mail

Most major companies have their own websites. Some information on these sites is useful, such as nutritional information about a product. But a company's website is mostly a large advertisement.

As a result, advertisers do all they can to bring people to their websites, by offering downloads, coupons, and contests. Brands with a young **target audience** will try to attract people to their website through social-networking sites. Many companies that target kids and teens offer games on their websites.

Advertisers hope that, once people visit, they will be influenced by the advertising on the website and will shop if there is a store. They also hope that visitors provide personal information when they register or fill out surveys. This will allow advertisers to contact these visitors with more advertising.

E-mail is another popular way for advertisers to reach consumers. Sometimes these e-mails can be useful—for example, if a store sends coupons. However, when these e-mails are not wanted, they can be annoying and are referred to as "spam." Spam can slow down computers and clutter people's in-boxes. As a result, spam-blocking software is being improved all the time. Many people also use their legal right and tell the company they want to "opt out" of future e-mails. This stops some, but not all, spam e-mail.

Banner and pop-up ads

Banner ads appear on the top, bottom, or sides of websites and search engines. They aim to get people's attention, often blinking, freezing, or flashing. Pop-up and pop-under ads pop on top of or under a web page. Advertisers hope that consumers not only see these ads, but also click on them and get led to their company website.

However, many people ignore banner ads; only about 1 percent are clicked on. As a result, some advertisers use "trick banners." These look like something important. They may look like a message from your operating system telling you to restart your computer. But once clicked on, they lead to a company website.

The annoyance caused by all these kinds of ads has led people to explore ad-blocking software.

Sponsored links

As people learn to ignore or block Internet advertising, advertisers are looking for "hidden" techniques. Sometimes search engines will provide links that look like search results, but are in fact paid advertisements. Advertisers pay search engines to make these **sponsored** links appear.

Sponsored links are often labeled "featured" or "sponsored" and are colored differently or placed separately from the actual search results. When you click on these links, you will probably see advertising.

Sometimes this is okay. If you are shopping for a certain product, a sponsored link might

Measuring success

With most media, advertisers cannot tell how effective an ad was—for example, how many people stopped and read a magazine ad. But with online advertising, advertisers can measure the success of an ad based on the number of times viewers click on it.

Spotting sponsors

Do a web search. Look at the sponsored links that appear. Are they similar to what you searched for? How can you tell the difference between your search results and the sponsored links?

take you to a site where the product is sold for a good price. But remember that there can be a big difference between a search result and an advertisement.

Viral marketing

Advertisers have recently had success online with **viral marketing**. This means creating an interesting idea (such as an event or game) on the Internet that gets people talking about a product or service.

For example, when the movie *The Dark Knight* came out in 2008, the movie company led fans on scavenger hunts across the Internet for clues to puzzles. Thousands of people spent hours unraveling and discussing the puzzles.

This kind of advertising generally creates positive feelings in consumers. It also creates a lot of fairly inexpensive advertising. Has viral marketing caused you to buy a product?

U.S. online advertising

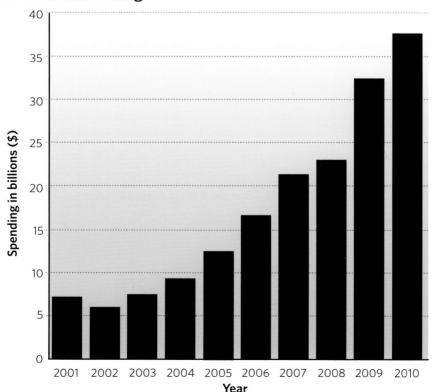

Controversies in advertising: Privacy concerns

Have you ever noticed that the banner and pop-up ads you see reflect your interests? Does it seem like advertisers know who you are? In a way, they do.

Major search engines and service providers like Google, Microsoft, and Yahoo! are moving toward "personalized services." They are trying to provide people with advertisements and information that reflect their individual interests. To do this, they keep a record of every time you type or click something. They also let advertising networks collect your private information. These advertising networks are responsible for placing ads, and they give your information to companies that want you to buy their products.

Some people think it is useful to have the Internet tailored to their interests. Advertisers argue that **free speech** allows them to reach consumers this way.

Other people worry that this is a huge invasion of privacy. If you search for topics about something personal, such as a medical or family problem, this information is out there for companies to access. Also, people worry about having information like credit card numbers accessible to others. This can lead to identity theft. This is when someone pretends to be another person and uses that individual's personal information to buy things or set up shady business dealings.

Software is being developed that will allow more privacy for users. Governments are also reviewing ways to better protect consumers' privacy. Knowing all this, will you be more selective in what you search for in the future?

Become a savvy consumer

As advertisers come up with newer (and sometimes stranger) techniques and media, who knows what will come next?

Do your best to become a **savvy** consumer. Sometimes you might genuinely be interested in hearing about a product, or you might enjoy a creative advertisement. But at the same time, think about the messages advertisers are sending to you. Be smart about the tricks advertisers use, and remember to look out for ads where you least expect them.

If you do not like what some advertisements are trying to do, you have power as a consumer. You can choose not to buy products from that company, or you can write letters to the company or to media such as a local newspaper.

You cannot create a world in which there is no advertising, but you can control how you respond to it.

 Be safe

Never give out your personal information to strangers in chat rooms or on social-networking sites. Talk to your parents before giving information on a company website.

Personal information includes things like your phone number, age, address, school, instant messaging name, and your last name.

The more information you give, the easier it is for others to find you or steal your personal information.

 If you use it wisely, the Internet can be a great resource.

Do-It-Yourself

As this book has shown, advertising is often a big business with huge **budgets**. However, anyone can use the **strategies**, techniques, and tricks of advertising.

In this activity, pretend that you are in charge of getting lots of people to attend a school dance. Use your knowledge of advertising to make an effective **advertising campaign** for the dance.

1   Think about what strategy you want to use to get the most people to come. Also think about the message you want the reader to get. You could make people feel that "everyone will be there," playing upon people's need to fit in. You could also use emotion, making it seem like the night will be an unforgettable memory. Or what about humor?

2   After you have chosen your strategy, begin your advertising campaign by making some posters. Think about how you can use words effectively. Can you come up with a clever **slogan** or name for the dance that will grab people's attention? Make sure the poster gives all the important details as well, such as the time, place, and appropriate dress.

3   Now think about how to use images. Will you use a photo of people dancing or draw a picture? What kind of people do you want to show—"perfect" people, or people who look like everyday students? This will be a part of your strategy.

4   Pull all the pieces of your poster together into a striking final design. Try to grab people's attention with a bold arrangement of images and bright colors, if possible.

By creating a poster advertising a dance, you will gain a better understanding of how advertisers do their jobs.

5 Once you have made many copies of your poster, think about where you will place them. What locations will lead to the maximum number of students seeing them?

6 Now try to extend your advertising campaign to different **media**. Using the same basic strategy and ideas as your poster, what other kinds of ads could you use—maybe stickers or postcards? What about placing a print ad in the school newspaper, or making an announcement on the school's intercom? If your school has an e-mail system or website, try online advertising as well.

You could also make chalk drawings outside as your own sort of **guerrilla marketing**. (Ask an adult first!) Think about **place-based advertising**. Maybe you could place posters and postcards in unexpected places like bathroom stalls.

An effective campaign will reach the most possible people.

Advertising Timeline

1760–1850 The Industrial Revolution, a period of rapid factory and powered-machine development, which changes everyday life in Europe and North America. These changes help push the development of advertising, as there are suddenly more products to advertise and buy.

1842 The first U.S. **advertising agency** is formed by Volney Palmer, in Philadelphia. Many see this as the beginning of modern advertising.

mid-1800s Early advertisers use **broadsides**, **trade cards**, and **handbills**. Newspapers and magazines are widely available and affordable. As a result, they become an important **medium** for advertisers. Advertising agencies become more common, acting as "middle men" who place ads in newspapers and magazines.

1870s A printing technique called lithography is perfected, allowing color and images into the printing process. This allows posters to become an important medium in advertising.

1880s Major companies begin to create packaging with **logos** and recognizable images. This leads to the importance of recognized brand names.

late 1800s Billboards are developed as an important advertising medium.
People begin to advertise patent medicines. These are medicines that falsely claim all sorts of positive effects in their advertisements. Many patent medicines actually do harm, as they contain alcohol or drugs like cocaine. These products lead to laws requiring more honesty in advertising.

1900 Large advertising agencies begin to form. These agencies begin to specialize in creating advertisements, in addition to placing them in major media.

1914 The Federal Trade Commission Act is passed in the United States, creating the Federal Trade Commission, which monitors advertising.

1920s Radio develops as a new medium for advertising. In the United States, early advertisers **sponsor** programs. At first advertisers get their names in the titles of shows—for example, the *Maxwell House Show Boat*—and have their product advertised throughout a program. This changes over time to a variety of different advertisers having commercials spread throughout a program.

1930s The Great Depression leaves many people with little money to spend. Advertisers get desperate and create ads that scare people into buying their products. As a result, laws are passed to require more honesty in advertising.

1940s Advertisers join the war effort for World War II (1939–45), creating **propaganda** in the form of posters, radio advertisements, and print advertisements.
Rosser Reeves creates the idea of the "Unique Selling Proposition." Television becomes an important new medium for advertisers. In the United States, companies at first sponsor entire shows, such as the *Kraft Television Theater*. Gradually this gives way to programs featuring a variety of ads from different companies.

1950s Major advertising agencies form on New York City's Madison Avenue. As people have more money to spend, these advertisers sell the idea of a perfect home full of new appliances and other products.

1960s Important new advertising agencies form in the United Kingdom and Europe.
Advertisers begin to pursue more creative, friendly approaches.

1976 The U.S. Supreme Court makes an important ruling that says that advertising is a form of **free speech**.

1980s Cable television becomes an important new medium for advertisers.
Advertisers have increasingly huge **budgets** to spend on worldwide **advertising campaigns**.

1990s The Internet becomes an important new medium for advertisers.

2000s In an effort to get **consumers'** attention, advertisers explore new ideas like **place-based advertising**, **guerrilla marketing**, **viral marketing**, **undercover marketing**, and more.
Advertisers spend increasing amounts of money on Internet advertising.

Glossary

advertising agency place where a group of people specialize in creating effective advertisements

advertising campaign overall advertising strategy for a product, including the various media it will appear in and the overall message communicated

advertorial print advertisement that is designed and written to seem like the newspaper or magazine articles that surround it

ambush marketing advertising technique in which advertisers show up at an event sponsored by a competitor's product to try to sell their own product

branding creating a strong image for a product

broadside type of large, printed piece of paper that was used before new printing techniques made posters popular

budget amount of money available to spend on something, such as an advertising campaign

commercialism spirit of focusing on buying and selling things

consumer person who buys things

fine print tiny print that appears at the bottom of advertisements, often hiding information that advertisers do not want consumers to notice

focus group people who are paid to tell their opinions about a product or advertisement

free speech right to speak your mind and not be silenced

guerrilla marketing advertising technique in which advertisers create a clever, attention-grabbing advertising campaign in a public place, usually using odd techniques that cost very little money

handbill piece of paper with information that is handed out or posted; also called a flyer

infomercial television commercial that seems like regular programming

insecurity feeling of not being good enough

logo words or symbols that represent a brand

marketing getting the message out about a product or service

medium (plural: media) place that information is provided, such as a newspaper

objective not representing someone's opinion; based on facts

place-based advertising advertising technique in which advertisers put advertisements in places where people will see them as they go about their everyday lives, such as bus shelters

product placement technique in which advertisers pay a medium such as a television show to show their product being used

propaganda advertising technique that makes people believe in a political cause, sometimes by glossing over some parts of the truth so as to make one side seem clearly in the right

savvy informed and educated

slogan memorable line used to advertise a product, such as "You deserve a break today" (McDonald's)

sponsor support something, such as a television show or sporting event, usually by giving it money

statistic number that reflects results from studies

status symbol product that suggests a person is wealthy or important

strategy idea for how to approach something and get specific results

target audience specific people an advertiser wants to reach

testimonial advertising technique in which an advertisement uses the voice or words of an everyday person offering a personal story about how a product or service worked for him or her

trade card small card describing a business's services

undercover marketing advertising technique in which people are paid to talk up a product while pretending to be everyday consumers

viral condition of something being spread across the Internet by being talked about in blogs and chat rooms

viral marketing advertising technique that creates an interesting idea (such as an event or game) on the Internet to get people talking about a product or service

Find Out More

Books

Adcock, Donald and Beth, Pulver. *Information Literacy Skills* (series). Chicago, IL: Heinemann Library, 2009.

Graydon, Shari. *Made You Look: How Advertising Works and Why You Should Know*. Paradise, CA: Paw Prints, 2008.

Mierau, Christina. *Accept No Substitutes!: The History of American Advertising*. Minneapolis, MN: Lerner, 2000.

Petley, Julian. *Media Wise: Advertising*. North Mankato, MN: Smart Apple Media, 2004.

Stanford, Eleanor, ed. *Introducing Issues with Opposing Viewpoints: Advertising*. San Diego, CA: Greenhaven, 2007.

Websites

"Don't Buy It: Get Media Smart"
http://pbskids.org/dontbuyit
This Public Broadcasting Service (PBS) website teaches young people how to be savvy consumers.

"Duke University Libraries: Ad* Access"
http://library.duke.edu/digitalcollections/adaccess/
Check out this Duke University website to see a wide range of advertisements from 1911 to 1955.

"Center for Media Literacy"
www.medialit.org
This website provides more information about understanding the way various media work.

"On Guard Online"
www.onguardonline.gov
Learn more about Internet safety at this website.

Place to visit

The William F. Eisner Museum of Advertising and Design

208 N. Water Street

Milwaukee, Wisconsin 53202

Phone: (414) 847-3290

www.eisnermuseum.org

Topics to research

To learn more about advertising, do research on the following topics:

- focus groups and consumer research
- copywriting and design in advertising
- advertising regulations

Index